# ROBOTS AND ROBOTICS

# Space Robots

## Tony Hyland

Smart Apple Media

Smart Apple Media
2140 Howard Drive West
North Mankato, Minnesota 56003

First published in 2007 by
MACMILLAN EDUCATION AUSTRALIA PTY LTD
15–19 Claremont Street, South Yarra, Australia 3141

Visit our Web site at www.macmillan.com.au or go directly to www.macmillanlibrary.com.au

Associated companies and representatives throughout the world.

Library of Congress Cataloging-in-Publication Data

Hyland, Tony.
   Space robots / by Tony Hyland.
   p. cm. — (Robots and robotics)
   Includes index.
   ISBN 978-1-59920-121-4
   1.  Space robotics—Juvenile literature.  I. Title.

   TL1097.H95 2007
   629.8'92—dc22

                                                    2007004746

Edited by Margaret Maher
Text and cover design by Ivan Finnegan, iF Design
Page layout by Ivan Finnegan, iF Design
Photo research by Legend Images

Printed in U.S.

## Acknowledgements
The author and the publisher are grateful to the following for permission to reproduce copyright material:

Front cover photograph: Artist's impression of the Mars Rover vehicle, courtesy NASA/JPL/Cornell University.

Photos courtesy of:
NASA, pp. 21, 27, 28, 29; NASA/ARES, p. 16; NASA/John Hopkins University APL/Southwest Research Institute, p. 25; NASA/JPL, pp. 7, 9, 13, 15, 22, 26; NASA/JPL-Caltech, p. 14; NASA/JPL/Craig Attebery, p. 23; NASA/JPL/Corby Waste, p. 4; NASA/JPL/Cornell University, pp. 1, 12; NASA/JSC, pp. 18, 19, 20; NASA Kennedy Space Center, p. 11; Photolibrary/GE Astro Space/Science Photo Library, p. 8; Photolibrary/David A. Hardy/Science Photo Library, p. 6; Photolibrary/NASA/Science Photo Library, p. 5; Photolibrary/Ria Novosti/Science Photo Library, p. 10; Photolibrary/Sam Ogden/Science Photo Library, p. 17; Photolibrary/US Naval Observatory/Science Photo Library, p. 24.

Background textures courtesy of Photodisc.
While every care has been taken to trace and acknowledge copyright, the publisher tenders their apologies for any accidental infringement where copyright has proved untraceable. Where the attempt has been unsuccessful, the publisher welcomes information that would redress the situation.

# Contents

**GLOSSARY WORDS**

When a word is printed in **bold**, you can look up its meaning in the glossary on page 31.

# Robots

There are more and more robots in the world. Once they were just figments of the imagination, metal creatures that clanked through old **science fiction** movies and books. Robots today are real, and you will find them in the most surprising places. Some are tiny, no bigger than a fly. Others are among the largest machines on Earth.

Robots are machines that can move and think for themselves. Most robots work in factories, doing endless, repeated tasks faster than any human. Other robots explore places that humans cannot safely reach. Some robots go to the bottom of the sea. Others go to the rocky surface of Mars.

There are also **surgical robots**, robots that carry out scientific experiments, and robots that **disarm** bombs. Today's toys often include robot technology—you can even **program** your own toy robot.

Where do robots fit into your life?

Earth's solar system.

*Mars Global Surveyor* is a robotic space explorer.

Neptune

Mars

Earth

Mercury

Uranus

# Space robots

There are many robots exploring space today. Some are **satellites** in **orbit** around Earth. Some are small space vehicles flying past the planets of our solar system. Several **rovers** have landed on Mars to explore its rocky surface.

Space is a dangerous place for humans. There is no air, food, or water. Astronauts can travel into space for short periods. However, they must take supplies of air, food, and water with them. Robots need none of these things. When they have finished their mission, they do not have to return to Earth. They can simply stay in space, instead of needing expensive return flights. For these reasons, robots almost always explore new areas before human astronauts do.

Plans for exploring space in the next few years all require robots to go into space first. Robots will land on the Moon, on Mars, and on the moons of Saturn and Jupiter long before humans do.

Jupiter

Venus

Saturn

Kuiper belt

The rover *Spirit* explored Mars for more than three years.

# The first space explorers

The earliest space explorers were not really robots. They did not have built-in computers, and were controlled by radio signals from Earth. In 1957, the Soviet Union launched *Sputnik 1*, the first satellite to orbit Earth. It sent back data about Earth's **atmosphere**.

Over the next few years, many more satellites were sent into orbit. Today, satellites and **space probes** are robotic. They are controlled by computers.

*Sputnik 1* was the first satellite to orbit Earth.

## Useful satellites

Some satellites, such as *Telstar*, were used for sending telephone and television communications around Earth. Others collected information on the weather. Satellites fitted with powerful cameras were used for making maps of Earth.

## ROBOFACT

### A MINIATURE SPUTNIK

Many *Sputnik* satellites went into orbit after 1957. In 1997, on the fortieth anniversary of *Sputnik 1*, *Sputnik 40* was launched. It was a model one-third the size of the original *Sputnik*.

# *Space probes*

Soon after the first satellites went into orbit, new space vehicles called probes were launched. Some of these probes took photos while in orbit. Others landed on the Moon and sent data back to Earth.

## Traveling through the solar system

In the late 1970s, **NASA** launched two *Voyager* probes. They traveled close to Jupiter and Saturn, and sent back amazing photos of the outer planets.

The two probes have now gone far past all the planets of our solar system. They have traveled farther than any other space vehicles. They still send back data to researchers on Earth. Scientists expect them to stop sending data in about 2030, when their batteries will run out completely.

## Signals at the speed of light

Radio signals travel at the speed of light, almost 187,000 miles per second. Yet space is so huge that radio messages to the *Voyager* probes take about 15 hours each way.

The *Voyager* space probes traveled beyond our solar system.

# Robots in orbit

Today, there are more than 400 space vehicles in orbit. They may not look like robots, but they do their work without human help. This means they really are robots.

## Orbiting Earth

Most satellites orbiting Earth have instruments pointed at Earth or other places in space. Communication satellites receive signals from different places and bounce them to other areas far away. Earth observation satellites take photographs and measurements to create maps. Astronomical satellites, such as the *Hubble Space Telescope*, observe distant planets and other space objects.

## Types of orbits

There are several types of orbit. Communication satellites stay in one place above Earth. This is called a **geosynchronous orbit**. Most other satellites orbit around Earth, making a full revolution every 90 minutes.

## ROBOFACT

### SPACE DEBRIS

After a few years, satellites run out of power and become useless **space debris**. There are over 8,000 pieces of space debris orbiting Earth.

Some satellites, such as *Astra-1B*, are used to broadcast satellite television.

# Orbiting other planets

Many space probes have been sent to orbit other planets. They take photographs and record other data, such as the surface temperature. Early **orbiters** were sent to the Moon, Venus, and Mercury. Orbiters over Venus discovered that it is a very hot planet.

## Studying Mars

Today, several vehicles are in orbit around Mars. This is mainly because Mars is the first planet that humans will visit, in about 2020. *Mars Express, Mars Odyssey, Mars Global Surveyor,* and *Mars Reconnaissance Orbiter* are all orbiting Mars. These robotic satellites are photographing the surface of Mars and sending data back to Earth.

Other orbiting satellites include *Messenger,* which will orbit Mercury from 2011. *Venus Express* is orbiting Venus. These modern space robots are far more advanced than the probes of the 1970s.

The *Mars Reconnaissance Orbiter* photographed the surface of Mars while orbiting the planet.

# Robot rovers

Robots that can land on the surface of a planet and move from place to place are called rovers. These robots help scientists learn about conditions on the planets.

## Lunokhod rovers

The first rovers were two *Lunokhod* rovers made by the Soviet Union in the 1970s. These two robots landed on the Moon. They were powered by **solar panels**, so they worked during the day and shut down at night. *Lunokhod 1* took 20,000 photographs and carried out many tests on the Moon's soil. *Lunokhod 2* took another 80,000 photographs. It traveled for more than 23 miles (37 km) across the Moon's surface.

The *Lunokhod* rover was the first robot to explore the Moon.

## ROBOFACT

### HOW BIG WERE THE LUNOKHOD ROVERS?

The *Lunokhod* rovers weighed over 1,850 pounds (840 kg) each. They were 53 inches (135 cm) high and 67 inches (170 cm) long. Each rover had eight wheels, with independent suspension, a motor, and a brake for each wheel. They traveled at about 1 mile (1.6 km) per hour.

# The first Martian rover

In 1997, NASA scientists sent a new rover to Mars. It was called *Sojourner*.

*Sojourner* was much smaller than the *Lunokhod* rovers. It weighed only 23 pounds (10 kg). Six independent wheels allowed it to travel across the rocky Martian surface.

*Sojourner* carried a television camera and still cameras. It used a grinder and other tools to **analyze** the Martian rocks and soil.

## *Sojourner* explores Mars

NASA scientists tried an unusual landing for *Sojourner*. It parachuted to the surface, protected inside a set of inflatable airbags. This system protected the rover from any harm.

*Sojourner* traveled several hundred yards over the next three months. Signals from Earth took about 20 minutes to reach Mars. This meant that controlling the rover was a slow and difficult task. *Sojourner's* built-in programs were designed to deal with emergencies, such as rolling into unexpected potholes.

NASA's *Sojourner* rover was the first robot to explore the surface of Mars.

# The new Mars rovers

In January 2004, two new rovers landed on Mars. *Spirit* and *Opportunity* were identical robots, sent to search for water.

## Six-wheeled robots

*Spirit* and *Opportunity* are large, six-wheeled robots. Each of their aluminum wheels is independent. This means the rovers can travel over rocks without tipping.

Both robots carry cameras, which they use to examine the ground. The pictures are beamed back to Earth. The rovers' onboard computers control their wheels and instruments.

## Solar power

The two rovers carry solar panels, so they can recharge their batteries. Eventually, the solar panels will become too dusty to gather energy. When this happens, the rovers will shut down.

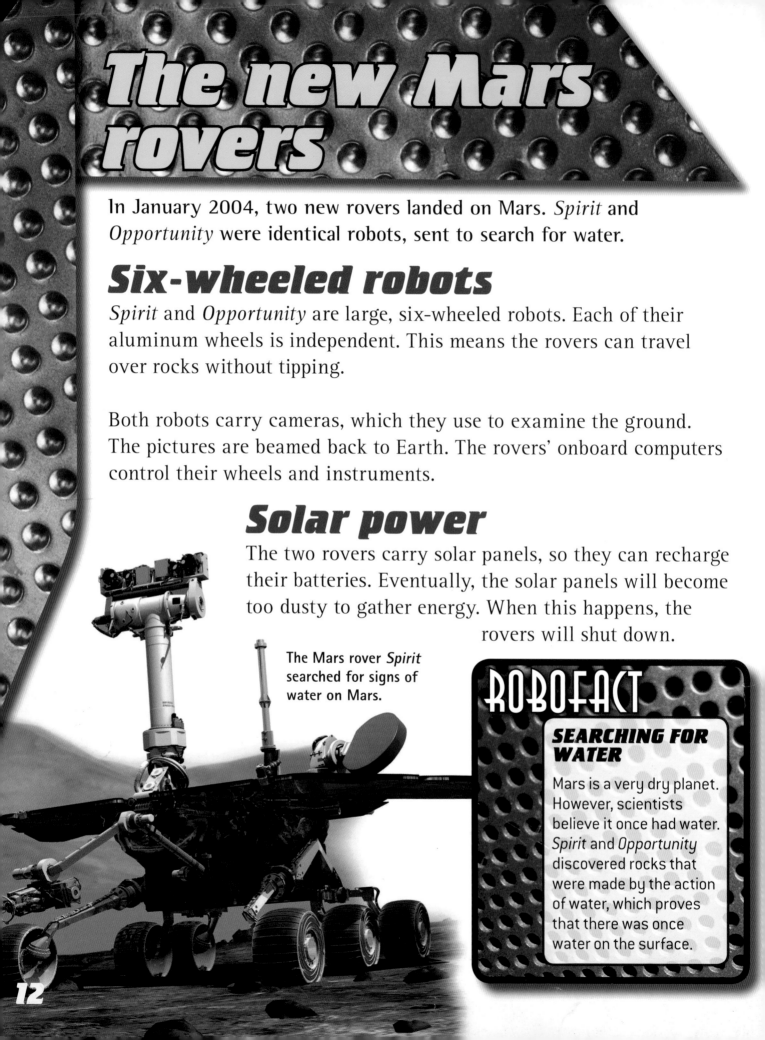

The Mars rover *Spirit* searched for signs of water on Mars.

## ROBOFACT

### SEARCHING FOR WATER

Mars is a very dry planet. However, scientists believe it once had water. *Spirit* and *Opportunity* discovered rocks that were made by the action of water, which proves that there was once water on the surface.

# Up Close

**ROBOT**
Mars Rover *Opportunity*

**JOB**
Exploring the surface of Mars

**MAKER**
NASA, U.S.

**SKILLS**
Driving over rocky and sandy ground, analyzing rocks

**SIZE**
63 inches (160 cm) long,
59 inches (150 cm) high

**WEIGHT**
410 pounds (186 kg)

*Opportunity* is one of two rovers which landed on Mars in January 2004. It is designed to find out more about Mars's surface.

NASA controllers direct the rover to interesting rocks and craters. *Opportunity* uses its built-in guidance system to control its exact movements.

In April 2005, the rover became stuck in a sand dune. NASA controllers took four weeks to free the rover. Eventually, *Opportunity* rolled free of the dune and went on its way.

*Opportunity* was designed to work for three months. However, it was so reliable that it worked well for more than three years. It traveled more than 5 miles (8 km) in that time.

# Future Mars explorers

Several more robots will be heading to Mars over the next few years. The first will be a **lander** named *Phoenix*.

## Searching for microbes

In May 2008, *Phoenix* will touch down on Mars. *Phoenix* is not a rover. It will stay in one place, digging trenches. Its robotic systems will test thousands of soil samples. *Phoenix* could find evidence of **microbes** living in the underground waters of Mars.

## A giant rover

In 2010, a new rover will land on Mars. The *Mars Science Lab* will be twice as long and three times as heavy as *Spirit* and *Opportunity*. It will have a built-in laser to analyze pieces of rock. This will tell scientists on Earth what the rocks are made of.

The *Mars Science Lab* rover is a larger version of *Spirit* and *Opportunity*.

## ROBOFACT

### WHERE'S THE MOTOR?

The NASA Mars rovers do not have a motor like a car. They are run by small electric motors inside each wheel.

# A return mission

The early robots that were sent on missions to Mars all stayed on the planet. NASA researchers have now designed a new set of robots. These robots will travel to Mars, collect samples, and return the samples to Earth.

## Sample collectors

The *Mars Sample Return* mission will land on Mars in about 2015. It will have a large landing vehicle, robotic rovers, and a small robotic **return vehicle**. The rovers will collect samples of rocks and soil with their robotic arms. They will place the samples into the return vehicle. When the return vehicle has enough samples, it will blast off from Mars and return to Earth.

## Test mission

The *Mars Sample Return* mission will be a good way for scientists to test the robots. If the system works, sample return missions will be sent to other planets. Robots will bring back samples before human astronauts ever reach the more distant planets.

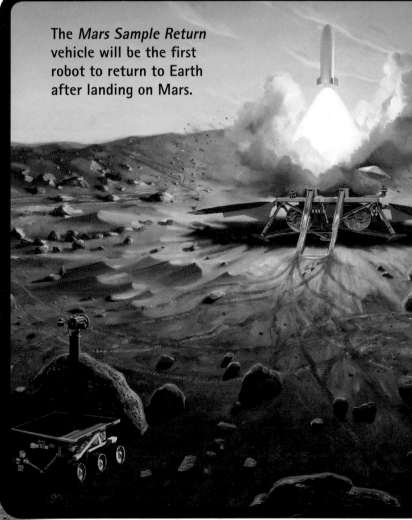

The *Mars Sample Return* vehicle will be the first robot to return to Earth after landing on Mars.

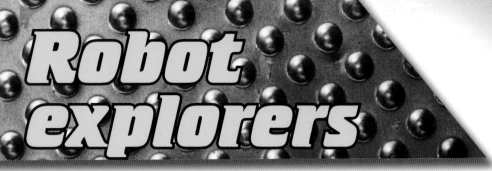

# Robot explorers

The robots that explore Mars over the next few years will be large rovers. However, scientists have developed many unusual robots that could be sent to Mars in the future.

## Flying robot

*ARES* is a flying robot that could be used to explore Mars from the air. It has a large wingspan area, as the Martian air is thin. The robot would be folded up for the journey from Earth. About 1 mile (1.6 km) above the Martian surface, *ARES* would unfold and fly. The robot would take photos and record other data. When it ran out of fuel, *ARES* would crash to the ground.

## ROBOFACT

### INTO THIN AIR

The atmosphere of Mars is very thin. This would make it impossible for normal airplanes to fly. There is not enough air to keep them up. *ARES* has huge, broad wings to help it to stay aloft.

*ARES* could fly above the surface of Mars to record information.

# Self-transforming robots

One team of scientists is developing self-transforming robots. These robots could pull themselves apart and reassemble themselves in new shapes. Self-transforming robots could travel to places that a rover could never reach. They could climb up tall cliffs or across ravines. They could build themselves into a ladder or a bridge. Other robots could then climb with their help.

A fish-shaped robot, such as *Robotuna*, could explore icy seas on the moons of Jupiter and Saturn.

# Fish-like robots

Some of the moons of Jupiter and Saturn are covered by icy seas. Robotics experts have designed robots that look like fish and seahorses to explore these seas. These robots are known as roboswimmers.

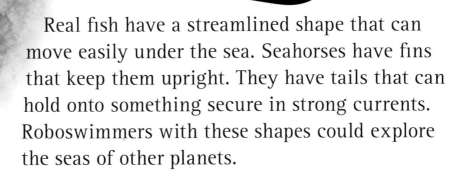

Real fish have a streamlined shape that can move easily under the sea. Seahorses have fins that keep them upright. They have tails that can hold onto something secure in strong currents. Roboswimmers with these shapes could explore the seas of other planets.

# Robonaut

Most of the robots working in space are wheeled rovers or flying vehicles. But Robonaut is about the size and shape of a human astronaut.

## Working with humans

Robonaut was designed to work with astronauts. It can do the work that they do. It can assemble sections of the **space station** or service satellites in orbit.

## Almost human

Robonaut is a **humanoid** robot. It has a head, fitted with several cameras. Its body contains most of its brain and mechanical controls. Robonaut's arms and hands are human-sized. It does not have legs, as it does not need them in space.

Robonaut is being tested in NASA laboratories.

## ROBOFACT

### JUST LIKE THE MOVIES?

Robonaut is a very advanced robot. However, it is nothing like the robots in science fiction movies. It is programmed to do only a few useful actions. It can recognize and answer some voice commands, but it could not have a conversation with its astronaut co-workers.

# Up Close

**ROBOT**
Robonaut

**JOB**
Working alongside human astronauts

**MAKER**
NASA, U.S.

**SKILLS**
Three-dimensional vision, obeying voice commands, using tools like a human

**SIZE**
About the size of a human

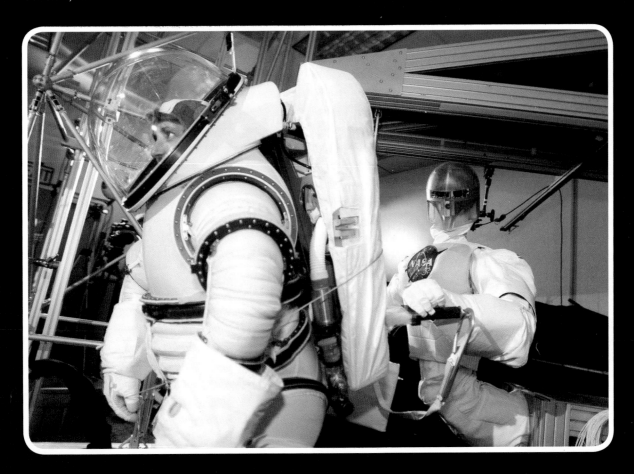

Robonaut has been designed to do the same jobs as human astronauts. It can work with astronauts, or it can take the place of astronauts in dangerous situations. Like most space robots, it does not work alone, but takes commands from a controller.

The most useful place for Robonaut to work is outside the space vehicle. This is a dangerous environment for humans. If anything goes wrong, a human astronaut could die within a few seconds.

Robonaut could take the place of a human for many of the tasks that must be done. For example, it could replace damaged equipment. Its hands can grasp tools and other objects, and adjust them to the correct tightness and position.

# Space station robots

Astronauts in the International Space Station are busy for long hours each day. Robots can help astronauts with many tasks.

## Robotic arm

The International Space Station has a huge robotic arm, called the Remote Manipulation System (RMS). The RMS can be used like a crane, to lift and carry equipment. It also has a platform. Astronauts can attach themselves to the platform when they are working outside the station.

## Robotic hand

The newest part of the RMS is a robotic hand. The hand is about 10 feet (3 m) long. Astronauts can use it to do jobs such as changing the space station's batteries. These batteries weigh about 220 pounds (100 kg) each.

## ROBOFACT

### FLOATING IN SPACE

Even the simplest action is difficult in space. When an astronaut tries to turn a bolt, the effort just spins the astronaut around. The RMS holds the astronaut steady so that this doesn't happen.

The RMS on the International Space Station helps astronauts stay safe when working outside the station.

# Robotic assistants

Several small, floating robots have been designed to work inside the space station. The robotic video camera called Sprint is about the size and shape of a basketball. The personal assistant robot called SPHERE is a similar size.

NASA astronauts helped test the SPHERE robot during its first trials.

## Sprint

Sprint can operate inside or outside the space station. It has 12 **thrusters** pointing in different directions. The thrusters push the robot in the direction it needs to go. They stop the robot when it is in position. Astronauts can use Sprint to inspect hard-to-reach places outside the space station.

## SPHERE

SPHERE looks similar to Sprint, but it only works inside the space station. It has six small fans inside to push it through the air. SPHERE is programmed to float beside an astronaut, giving directions on difficult tasks. It can read out instructions to the astronauts, and respond to voice commands.

# Exploring the solar system

The solar system is so large that voyages to the more distant planets take years. Robotic space vehicles are the only way that we can explore these planets.

## Orbiting robots

In the 1970s, the *Voyager* probes traveled past the outer planets of our solar system. They took photos and sent back data. More recently, robotic probes traveled to Mars. The *Mars Reconnaissance Orbiter* went into orbit around Mars in 2006. It took high definition photos of the planet's surface.

The planets Jupiter and Saturn each have several large moons. Robotic probes will spend many years flying around each of these moons. The *Jupiter Icy Moons Orbiter* will launch in 2015. It will circle each of Jupiter's ice-covered moons for about a year.

## ROBOFACT

### NUCLEAR-POWERED PROBE

The *Jupiter Icy Moons Explorer* will be the first nuclear-powered space vehicle. It will have 100 times more power than any other space vehicle.

The *Jupiter Icy Moons Explorer* will use nuclear power. It will also have solar panels to collect solar energy.

# Up Close

**ROBOT**
*Cassini-Huygens*

**JOB**
Exploring Saturn and its moons

**MAKER**
NASA, the European Space Agency, and the Italian Space Agency

**SKILLS**
Taking detailed scientific measurements

**SIZE**
22 feet (7 m) tall,
13 feet (4 m) wide

**WEIGHT**
4,700 pounds (2,130 kg)

**SPECIAL FEATURE**
Detachable **lander** to explore Saturn's moon, Titan

This robotic probe is the largest probe ever sent into space. It was launched in 1997. It consisted of a spacecraft—*Cassini*—which carried a small lander called *Huygens*.

*Cassini-Huygens* traveled past Jupiter before heading to Saturn. In 2004, *Huygens* was launched from *Cassini* to land on Saturn's largest moon, Titan. *Huygens* parachuted to the ground, sending data back as it traveled through Titan's atmosphere.

Once *Huygens* was launched, *Cassini* continued toward Saturn. It is traveling in a complex path that will take it to each of Saturn's moons. *Cassini* has discovered three small moons that astronomers had never seen before.

# Exploring the outer planets

The most distant planets of our solar system are Jupiter, Saturn, Uranus, and Neptune. Any trip to these planets would take several years. Humans will not be able to visit these planets, unless we can build much faster spaceships. In the meantime, robots will be the explorers.

## Galileo

The *Galileo* probe traveled to Jupiter, reaching it in 1995 after a six-year journey. On its way, *Galileo* traveled near the **asteroid** belt between Mars and Jupiter. It was the first probe to go near asteroids. *Galileo* flew around Jupiter for eight years, recording thousands of photographs. When its mission was complete, NASA controllers deliberately crashed it into Jupiter's atmosphere, where it burned up.

*Galileo* released a smaller probe near Jupiter to collect information about Jupiter's atmosphere.

## ROBOFACT

### PASSING THE OUTER PLANETS

The *Voyager 2* probe passed Uranus in 1986 and Neptune in 1989. No other probe has been near these planets.

# Voyage to Pluto

A new robotic probe, *New Horizons*, was launched toward the dwarf planet Pluto in 2006. It will arrive in 2015. From Pluto, it will head out to explore the Kuiper Belt. This is an area with many large asteroids and other objects.

*New Horizons* is a small probe, about the size and shape of a grand piano. It is filled with the most advanced electronics available.

## Energy and communication

*New Horizons* will travel so far from the Sun that solar panels will not be able to collect any energy. Instead, the probe is powered by **plutonium**. Because of the extreme cold, the probe is heavily insulated with **thermal blankets**.

The robot will be so far from Earth that messages will take more than five hours to reach it. Controllers will direct the probe, but its computers will need to make decisions about its movements.

*New Horizons* is covered with thermal blankets to protect it from freezing temperatures in space.

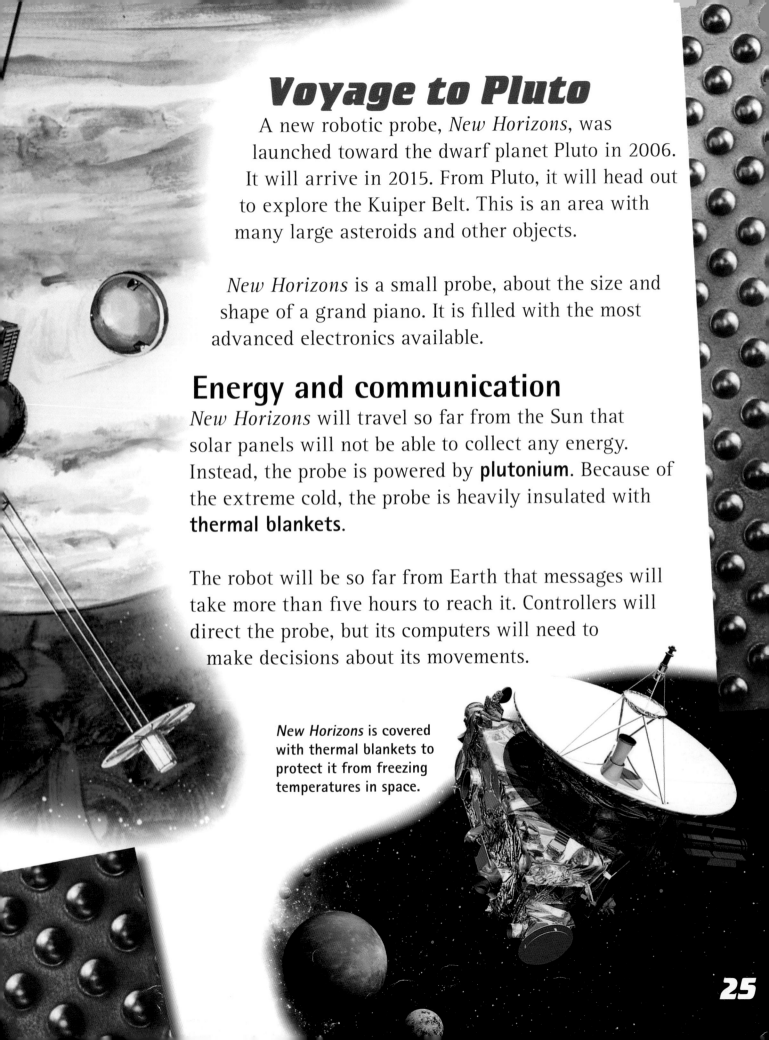

Most robots in space research work as single machines, exploring space or the surface of a planet. However, teams of robots will soon be used to prepare bases for future human landings.

## To the Moon and Mars

The United States plans to send astronauts to the Moon by 2020. After this, other astronauts will be sent to Mars. Before they arrive, teams of robots will be sent to construct buildings for the astronauts.

## Working together

The robot teams will need a range of abilities that no robots have had before. They will need to lift and carry sections of buildings, and then assemble them. They will also need to communicate and cooperate with each other.

### ROBOFACT

#### TEAMWORK

When two people lift something heavy, they cooperate to plan the job. As the item is lifted, each person naturally adjusts grip and balance. Today's robots cannot work together like this. They are not programmed to make adjustments and communicate the way humans do.

Robotic construction crews are being developed by NASA.

# Teamwork in the future

Teams of robots will become more important in space research in the future. They will be able to work together to get jobs done in a shorter time.

NASA scientists are developing new space robots to send to Mars. They try the robots out in sandy, rocky pits. These pits are made to look like the surface of Mars. Researchers give the robots tasks they will do on Mars, such as carrying equipment. Eventually, teams of robots will work on tasks such as erecting shelters.

## Can robot teams work?

Robot researchers are programming robots to work in teams. Robots that work together need to be able to see each other. They must be able to communicate, and know when the other robots are ready. They must also be able to continue working if one of the team members is damaged. When the astronauts arrive, the robots need to work with them as well.

On future expeditions to Mars, astronauts and robots will work as a team.

# Robotic exploration in the future

Humans will continue to explore space in the future, and robots will always be important. They can go to places and do things that humans will never be able to do.

## Robot explorers on outer planets

NASA intends to send humans to Mars soon after 2020, with the help of robots. But long before humans travel beyond Mars, there will be robotic explorers on the outer planets.

These robots will need to be very intelligent. They will be too far away for humans to control them. Controllers on Earth will direct them, but the robots will have to do the jobs independently.

NASA's *Deep Drill Lander* will be able to drill deep into the surface of Mars.

## ROBOFACT

### AROUND THE SUN

*Solar Orbiter* is a European probe that will fly to orbit the sun in 2015. It is expected to take images ten times sharper than the ones that we can take today.

# Robonauts of the future

Robonaut is ready to use in space now. However it will only be working on missions close to Earth, such as repairing satellites in orbit. Robonauts of the future will be much more advanced. They may travel farther into space and do much more complex jobs.

# Searching for new planets

One of the most exciting projects for space research is the search for planets outside our own solar system. We cannot travel the immense distances required to reach other solar systems. The journey would take many human lifetimes. However, by 2020, NASA plans to build huge telescopes in space to search for distant planets. Robot astronauts could work as helpers for the astronauts who build these telescopes.

Will we ever see space robots that look or act like the robots of *Star Wars*? It may happen, but it is many years in the future.

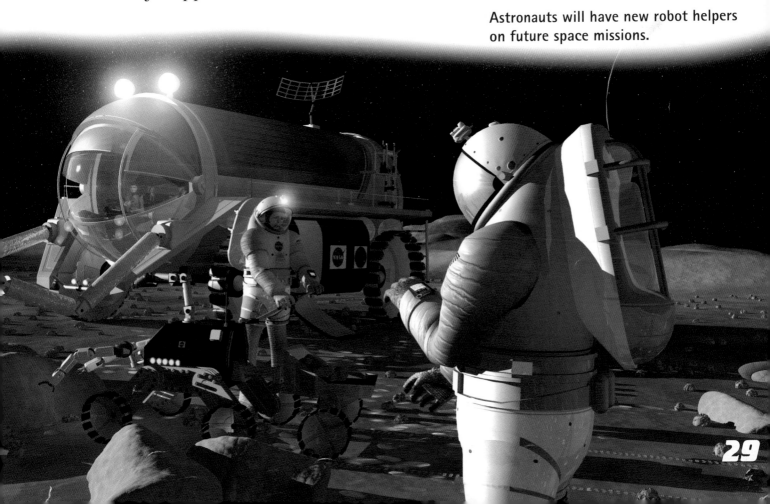

Astronauts will have new robot helpers on future space missions.

# Make a model Mars rover

If you have access to a Lego Mindstorms kit, you can create something that works like a robotic rover.

## What you need

- A Lego Mindstorms programming brick.
- Lego Technics pieces or other model pieces that will fit.
- A computer and the Lego software to program your robot. You can find lots of programs in books and on the Internet.

## What to do

1. Prepare your model with the brick as the body of the rover.
2. Include three axles and six wheels.
3. Add an arm to the brick.
4. Use the instructions in the kit to program the robot to roll forward.
5. Program the robot to stop and turn back when it hits a white line.

To get the most from your robot, work with friends or classmates. You might like to build a robot that can compete in the Robocup Junior program.

## Robocup Junior

Robocup Junior is a competition for school students. Teams of students build robots to compete in three sections: Robot Soccer, Robot Rescue, and Robot Dance.

The most appropriate section for a Mars rover is the Robot Rescue program. You can find out more through the Robocup Junior Web site.

Have fun!

# Glossary

**analyse** - to examine in close detail

**asteroid** - a small, rocky object orbiting the Sun

**atmosphere** - the layer of gases that surrounds a planet

**disarm** - to make an unexploded bomb safe

**geosynchronous orbit** - an orbit that matches Earth's rotation, so that the satellite remains above a certain point on Earth

**humanoid** - similar in shape to a human

**lander** - a space vehicle designed to land safely on another planet

**microbes** - microscopic living organisms, such as bacteria

**NASA** - National Aeronautics and Space Administration; the U.S. space agency

**orbit** - to revolve around a planet or other object in space

**orbiters** - space vehicles designed to orbit a planet or other object in space

**plutonium** - a radioactive substance similar to uranium

**program** - to install the instructions that control a robot's actions

**return vehicle** - a space vehicle designed to land on another planet and then return to Earth

**rovers** - robots designed to explore the surface of another planet

**satellites** - objects in orbit around a planet or other body in space

**science fiction** - stories based on futuristic scientific ideas

**solar panels** - large flat panels used to capture energy from the sun

**space debris** - the remains of rockets, satellites, and other objects in orbit around Earth

**space probes** - unmanned space vehicles that collect data about other planets

**space station** - a large orbiting spacecraft where humans can live and work for long periods of time

**surgical robots** - robots capable of performing surgical operations

**thermal blankets** - blankets designed to keep a space vehicle warm in extreme cold

**thrusters** - small rockets that push a robot or space vehicle in a chosen direction

# Index